Cybercrime –
A Criminological Perspective

Tansif ur Rehman

ELIVA PRESS

ELIVA PRESS

Tansif ur Rehman

Cybercrime is dissimilar as well as comparatively more atrocious than traditional crimes. It is evident that as ICT is expanding, cybercrime is also increasing exponentially. This expansion brings a lot of changes as well as transformations from conventional strategies to electronic means. Research encompassing cybercrime will be an important area to investigate, as society has evolved in being more dependent on technology. The rewards for even simple cybercrime can be immense for what is relatively little effort. The advancement of technology will certainly lead to a transformation of cybercrime which is why, some prefer to think of cybercrime as an ever changing set of behavior. One should be careful not to overestimate the potential harm of cybercrime. Where, technology could be programmed to be beneficial, it could equally programmed to be harmful. Author's intention is to critically view the adverse effects of cybercrime on individual's life as well as on society. In contemporary era, this work to an extent, will assist in understanding the modus operandi behind cybercrime and its repercussions.

Published: Eliva Press SRL
Address: MD-2060, bd.Cuza-Voda, 1/4, of. 21 Chişinău, Republica
Moldova
Email: info@elivapress.com
Website: www.elivapress.com

ISBN: 978-1-63648-019-0

Table of contents

Chapter 1: Cybercrime and Criminological Theories

Abstract

Cybercrime is a modern breed of crime and is executed by means of computers. It is dissimilar as well as comparatively more atrocious than traditional crimes. The crime is committed through an electronic mean, which makes it even complex to track as well as to recognize the relevant offender. It is evident that as ICT technology is expanding, cybercrime is also increasing exponentially. This expansion brings a lot of changes as well as transformations from conventional strategies to electronic means. For social science research, social theory provides an interface for conceptual clarity of the subject matter, which a researcher is pursuing. This interface develops perception and ideas of the researcher, which provides him maneuverability within the arena of social research. Research encompassing cybercrime will be an important area to investigate, as society has evolved in being more dependent on technology. The presented research has incorporated criminological theories and the respective research builds a context around these theories.

Keywords: *anonymity, criminology, cybercrime, cyberworld, cyberstalking, hacking, theories*

Introduction

"Cybercrime is a crime committed by means of computers or the internet" (Collins English Dictionary, 2020). While according to The Chambers Dictionary (2020), "Criminal activity or a crime that involves the internet, a computer system, or computer technology".

Encyclopedia Britannica (2020) states, "Cybercrime, the use of a computer as an instrument to further illegal ends, such as committing fraud, trafficking in child pornography and intellectual property, stealing identities, or violating privacy. Cybercrime, especially through the Internet, has grown in importance as the computer has".

According to Merriam-Webster (2020), "Criminal activity (such as fraud, theft, or distribution of child pornography) committed using a computer especially to illegally access, transmit, or manipulate data". While, in accordance with Oxford Advanced Learner's Dictionary (2020), "Crime that is committed using the internet, for example by stealing somebody's personal or bank details or by infecting their computer with a virus".

It is sometime tempting to downplay cybercrime, painting it always being the action of a lone individual, but while this is true of some crimes, the reality of cybercrime as a whole is very different (Benson & McAlaney, 2019; Johansen, 2020; Troia, 2020; Yar & Steinmetz, 2019). In contemporary era, several thousand groups are dedicated to cybercrime because of the rewards attached to it (Austin, 2020; Gillespie, 2019; Leukfeldt & Holt, 2019). It is clearly evident that as people become more dependent on technology, they become easier targets of cybercrime (Hudak, 2019; Martellozzo & Jane, 2017; Steinberg, 2019), as it also could evolve to bring about new problems (Hufnagel & Moiseienko, 2019; Marion & Twede, 2020). It is also important to realize to what extent it is understood by people that either they are really a victim or can be the victim of a cybercrime (Abaimov & Martellini, 2020; Marsh & Melville, 2019).

It is important to realize to what extent cybercrime is understood by people that either they are really a victim or can be the victim of a cybercrime (Azevedo, 2019; Carlson, 2019; Steinberg, 2019). For example, the sending of emails trying to influence people to enter their bank detail is illegal, but almost every one with an email address will have received an email asking them to confirm their bank details (Bancroft, 2019; Bandler & Merzon, 2020).

Another problem is the issue in identifying victims of cybercrime are those situations where people do not know that they have been victimized (Edwards 2019; Graham & Smith, 2019; Hutchings, 2013; Sangster, 2020). Most users of the computer will be aware of the need to install firewall and antivirus software (Littler & Lee, 2020; Schober & Schober; 2019). It is often rare for someone to be told that the program has stopped a virus or potential hack (Kim, 2018; Lavorgna, 2020; Willems, 2019).

According to Merton (1967), social theory refers to a logically interrelated set of propositions from which scientific uniformities are derived. A theory incorporates a handful speculation from which scientific generalizations have themselves been a derivative.

Similarly, social theory makes way to ease the understanding of the observation in an organized manner (Scott & Marshall, 2005). Moreover, social theories are inherently based on facts, and it facilitates to trace the respective social patterns. It not only gives a clear idea of society, but it is diverse in nature, because every social theory does not necessarily meet the fundamentals of every society that exists. For this reason, it can be said that, there is no single social theory that is available to describe every social phenomenon.

This means, that social research also clarifies and reformulates social theories and there remains interconnection between the two. It is imperative that the researcher is well oriented simultaneously with theoretical and conceptual aspects of the respective research problem. By following an approach of the 'pertinence of theory' the pursuit of research problem becomes systematic and fruitful.

Focus of the Research

The respective research encompasses the enlisted criminological theories with reference to behavior encompassing cybercrime in the contemporary era.

1. Frustration-Aggression Theory

2. General Strain Theory

3. Situational Crime Prevention Theory

Research Methodology

The basis of the study is based on the theoretical framework. At this point, a descriptive research methodology was used in the study. Descriptive research "is more concerned with what it is, rather than how or why it is something and aims to define a phenomenon and its properties" (Nassaji 2015, p.129).

Frustration-Aggression Hypothesis Theory

Dollard, et al. (1939) researched on aggression and presented their concise monograph on the subject matter. Their findings later on generally recognized as the frustration-aggression hypothesis (FA). Their interpretation of aggression, its logical as well as empirical consequences established to have a tremendous impact. It becomes evident that frustration-aggression

4

hypothesis have impacted the conventional thinking of West more than any other publication, due to its intellectual depth and insight.

According to Zillmann (1979), Frustration-aggression hypothesis has been providing guiding information that leads and direct the developmental study on aggression for more than thirty years.

Dollard et al. (1939) while developing a compendious theory of aggression, stated that the incitation and provocation that lead to aggression, is a function of below mentioned rationale :

a) Evaluating the response of the person's frustrated goal that intended to make that person more likely to behave aggressively.

b) The height of frustration escalating in response to reaching the ideal objective.

c) An extended series of frustrated reaction or response.

The respective propositions are candid as well as precised, specially the first two. The truculent attitude that augments aggravation is likely to escalate with the impetus, that could be attained or the feeling of repugnance that could be round out by the blocked goal response. While, the third proposition is not that considerable, until it is taken for granted or assumed that annoyance in behaviour, which is a result of frustration, increases in severity with repetition.

Although, the concept may not be easy to define precisely, most social psychologists have agreed to elaborate the concept of aggression as being a behavior aimed towards a specific goal. Certain features of the internet, though, may result in people being more likely than with other media to be exposed to material that they did not necessarily seek out. For example, a child attempting to gather information on the internet for a book report and typed the phrase 'little women' was connected to various pornography sites.

Social psychologists are fascinated by the fact that a vast range of people, depending on the situation, can participate in various forms of aggression (see Malamuth, Addison, & Koss, 2000). On a continuum of behavior ranging from verbal assaults to extreme forms of physical violence, a widely used distinction is between hostile and instrumental aggression (Geen, 2001).

Instrumental-aggression stress that harm is used primarily as a tactical mean for achieving goals, like money as well as social status. Typically, the definition of hostile-aggression stress that the primary goal is destruction, i.e. in form of injury or harm to respective target (Berkowitz, 1993).

These definitions and distinctions are especially important when thinking about aggression and the internet. As certain characteristics of the internet result in some forms of aggression being rare and other forms much more common.

A discussion of aggression and the internet cannot be limited to a consideration of only extreme forms of violence, such as homicide with guns, or terrorism with explosives, committed directly against a victim. Aggression as being a psychosocial aspect accomplished through a communication medium of the internet is often both subtler as well as encompassing, what we recognize as aggression on the social media.

Internet often has little to do with directly hitting, stabbing, or shooting. For example, aggression from senders whose identities are shielded may take the form of written or audio-verbal messages designed to hurt or humiliate. Indirect-aggression (Lagerspetz, Bjorkqvist, & Peltonen, 1988), which may take such forms as telling lies or stealing in the form of destructive messages, codes, 'viruses' or 'worms' designed to hinder or destroy others' work or computer software, also occurs. While, hate words are often used to incite individuals that are usually obscure and unfamiliar to one who composes it. Hate words are used to urge individuals to engage in aggressive behavior.

Attempts are now routinely made to steal identities and credit information from victims who are never seen. In all these cases, the broad definition of aggression would still apply because of the intention to harm the victim. The respective aspects of the internet that might support aggression can be organized in framework of general nature, as prescribed by social learning theorists, especially those theorists who focus on causes of aggressive behaviors (like Bandura, 1973, and 1977).

General Strain Theory

According to General Strain Theory, the negative emotions of humans, like feeling of displeasure and aggravation, is a result of strains or stimulus that causes stress. These negative emotions induce coercion for a mandatory action, which is one of the potential cause for the person to commit crime (Agnew, 1992).

Indulgence of a person in a criminal act is a possible procedure or process for mitigating excessive physical or mental tension, i.e. strain. For example, taking the money of another wrongfully for one's craving, may inflict injury or insult in return and may lessen an individual's negative feeling or emotions through substance or drug abuse. Most recent researches on the respective subject establish a strong relationship of many specific strains of the same category regarding crime and delinquency (Agnew, 2001; Aseltine, Gore, & Gordon, 2000; Mazerolle et al., 2000).

Conventionally, relationships in which others do not treat the individual as he or she would like to be treated cause frustration. Broidy and Agnew (1997), along with Elder, George, and Shanahan (1997), further elaborated in their propositions that, incidence like physical assault and conditions, like inadequate food and shelter is often regarded with dislike by most of the humans. While, other happenings and circumstances are assessed and valuate with groups distinguishing traits and qualities, such as gender and age, as their evaluation varies accordingly.

Patchin and Hinduja (2011) in their seminal work are of the view that Agnew's Strain Theory propounded that strain conditions usually results in negative feelings and sentiments. There may be many consequences of the situation including crime and delinquency. The particular strains which are argued in the General Strain Theory, include the failure of a person to accomplish positively valued goal, e.g money. The absence of a positive stimulant that directly influence the behaviour, e.g., loss of a valuable property, and the presence of negatively valued stimulant, e.g., physical or emotional abuse.

Agnew (1992; 2001) further elaborated strain as it is not the direct reason or influencer for the commission of crime but stimulate and elevate the negative human emotions like aggression and frustration. It is confluence directly with the Frustration-Aggression Hypothesis by Dollard et. al., (1939). These researchers hold an opinion that expression of anger comes before frustration, and frustration can be perceived into both aggressive and non-aggressive behavior (Runions, 2013)

As a reaction, the negative emotional behavior compel to cover up the responses to ease the mental pressure. To mitigate the psychological burden of deviancy and outrage, justified by the juvenile, as their resources are limited and the incapability to avoid the exasperating surrounding and environment.

General Strain Theory shows the logical relationship of unlawful behavior among children, like cyber bullying which is very much prevalent among them. The issue of cyber bullying is getting serious and its growth has invoked the authorities to take urgent notice globally.

It is a type of bullying that takes place with the help of digital devices, like cell phones, computers, and tablets. SMS, Text, and apps, social media, online gaming sites are few of the many forum which provide the platforms to deviants for bullying others.

Online activities have some distinguish properties which facilitate cyber bullying, i.e. no physical presence is required over the site, such as, anonymity, scale, global reach, availability, etc. Internet and technological advancement has made victims vulnerable to cyber criminals who can attack 24/7, and their anonymity will remain, as virtuality makes it difficult to identify and investigate them (Patchin & Hinduja, 2011).

Agnew (1992;2001) opined that strain causes anger, frustration and most of the time depression in people. Victim on the other hand, feels psychological inducement for the remedy. It seems as a corrective measure to victim in reaction, to mitigate the irritative feelings.

Therefore, as availability of technology is so common and easy, the victim finds cyber bullying as a justified action, that juvenile might take to lessen the irritative and bad feelings (Patchin & Hinduja, 2011).

Situational Crime Prevention Theory

According to Clarke (1980), the fundamental abstract of Situational Crime Prevention Theory is mitigating the favorable circumstances for criminal to commit crime. This theory can be considered peculiar as the discussion and arguments are focused on the commission of criminal event. The causative factors, like how offender got success in committing a crime? What were the methodologies and tactics used by the criminal?

According to Freilich and Newman (2016); Newman (1997); and Tilley (2004), this practical knowledge can be used to develop policies and measures to obstruct the criminal and mitigation of favorable environment for offender, so that the prevention can be ensured. It eschews abstruse motive or initiation of comprehensive actions to change or transform the attitude of the society

Freilich and Natarajan (2009) discussed in their work that Ronald Clarke (1980), significantly elaborated the importance of understanding situational factors, prone opportunities, and preventive measures, while establishing his theory of Situational Crime Prevention.

Hinduja and Kooi (2013) discussed the Situational Crime Prevention Theory in their proposition that, it is an elaborative work, which emphasize and direct on the preventive measures to negotiate distinct crimes, the management and utilization of skills to design the environment, so that it increases the risks and reduce the bounty or reward for the criminals.

The emphasis elaborated in Situational Crime Prevention Theory is on the reduction of favorable environment for the mitigation of crime, instead of focusing on criminals. The preventive measures are most important aspect of this theory. It is unlike to other criminological theories, where the strategy of criminals is of least significance. The SCP expresses the concern to design the physical environment for the crime prevention, rather focusing on criminal intentions or reasons of crime.

Most importantly, it looks for the measures which cause hurdles and difficulties for criminal to commit offense in their initiation process. Which, like other crime prevention strategies, aims to mitigate the vulnerabilities and opportunities, rather than focusing on the other aspects like bio-social, psychological aspects, etc. of the criminal.

According to Hinduja and Kooi (2013), these aspects can prevent cybercrime:

1.Target hardening

2.Controlling facilitators

3.Deflecting offenders

4.Access control

The concept of hardening the opportunities are both applicable in physical and cyberworld. For instance, installation of antivirus and firewall, etc. are the first line of defense in IT infrastructure. Developing the security culture in the organization where every employee routinely go through assessment and are restricted or educated regarding Bring Your Own Devices (BYOD) and unauthorized use of software, etc.

Divergence or deviation methods for criminals in the cyberworld are the measures which turn aside the criminal from a straight and easy offense, like hacking. One of the strategy, for example, is storing classified data to some other remote place where it gets harder for the offender to search and breach. Likewise, strategies for physical control is installation of CCTV cameras or access control are effective in restricting the criminal to access the sensitive area, e.g. server room, etc.

Hinduja and Kooi (2013) in their proposition highlighted the effectiveness of situational crime prevention strategies. Online crimes, like cyberstalking, identity theft, hacking, etc. can be well protected by the effective application of SCP fundamental assumptions. Other researches also reveal the importance of situation crime prevention strategies, that are not only helpful in preventing cybercrime, but also an effective deterrence for the cyber criminals, if applied effectively.

Solutions and Recommendations

1. General public awareness programs should be initiated with regards to cybercrime.

2. A strong global cyber force is required who can counter cyber threats.

3. Students should be educate regarding the vulnerabilities of cyberworld.

4. International conferences should be conducted at official level, where debates and issues pertaining the virtual world should be discussed.

5. At domestic level, special task force should be developed to ensure routine checks at the facilities where public internet access is available.

6. Websites should be under strict control regarding the offensive content.

7. Scholars should discuss cybercrime issue on different forums, specially in print as well as electronic media.

8. Criminological courses focusing on cybercrime should also be included in the regular studies of IT, social science education, law studies, business studies, etc.

Future Research Directions

Significant areas for conducting future research encompassing cybercrime via engaging qualitative, qualitative, or eclectic approach can be:

1. Causes of low reporting of cybercrime cases

2. Cybercrime and freedom of speech

3. Issues of gender and technology adaptability

4. Low conviction rates of cyber criminals

Conclusion

Cybercrime's pace in the global context is on a high rise. It is an offense that is even harder to identify and resolve as compared to traditional crimes. It is also important to realize to what extent it is understood by people that either they are or can be the victim of a cybercrime. This research emphasized on the aspects of integrating the traditional criminological theories encompassing crime to the context with regards to which cybercrime is committed by the criminals. These respective theories also presented a point of view as well as hypothesized regarding the basic causes of crime. This equips the readers with the very fact that why certain individuals compromise themselves as well as their social environment. Together, Frustration-Aggression Theory, and General Strain Theory provide an understanding of how people, especially youth, respond and deal with negative strain. Whether, it is to bully others or engage in deviant acts to alleviate the respective strain. If used effectively, the basic principles of Situational Crime Prevention Theory seems to be able to prevent most types of cybercrime in the contemporary era.

References

Abaimov, S., & Martellini, M. (2020). *Cyber arms security in cyberspace.* Boca Raton, CRC Press. ISBN: 9780367853860

Agnew, R. (1992). Foundation for a general strain theory of crime and delinquency. *Criminology, 30,* 47-87.

Agnew, R. (2001). An overview of general strain theory. In R. Paternoster & R. Bachman (Eds.), *Explaining criminals and crime.* LA: Roxbury Publishing Company.

Aseltine, R. H., Gore, S., & Gordon, J. (2000). Life stress, anger and anxiety, and delinquency: An empirical test of general strain theory. *Journal of Health and Social Behavior, 41,* 256-75.

Austin, G. (2020). *National cyber emergencies: The return to civil defence.* London, Routledge. ISBN: 9780367360344

Azevedo, F. U. B. (2018). *Hackers exposed: Discover the secret world of cybercrime.* Independently published. ISBN-13: 978-1718124615

Bancroft, A. (2019). *The darknet and smarter crime: Methods for Investigating criminal entrepreneurs and the illicit drug economy (Palgrave studies in cybercrime and cybersecurity).* Cham, Palgrave Macmillan.

Bandler, J., & Merzon, A. (2020). *Cybercrime investigations: A comprehensive resource for everyone.* CRC Press.

Bandura, A. (1973). *Aggression: A social learning analysis.* Englewood Cliffs, NJ: Prentice-Hall.

Bandura, A. (1977). *Social learning theory.* Englewood Cliffs, NJ: Prentice-Hall.

Benson, V., & McAlaney, J. (2019). *Emerging cyber threats and cognitive vulnerabilities* (1st ed.). Academic Press. ISBN-13: 978-0128162033

Berkowitz, L. (1993). *Aggression: Its causes, consequences, and control.* Philadelphia, PA: Temple University Press.

Broidy, L., & Agnew, R. (1997). Gender and crime: A general strain theory perspective. *Journal of Research in Crime and Delinquency, 34,* 275-306.

Carlson, C. T. (2019). *How to manage cybersecurity risk: A security leader's roadmap with open fair.* Universal Publishers.

Clarke, R. V. G. (1980). Situational crime prevention: Theory and practice. *The British Journal of Criminology, 20*(2), 1.

Cybercrime. (2020). In *Collins English Dictionary.*
https://www.collinsdictionary.com/dictionary/english/cybercrime

Cybercrime. (2020). In *Encyclopedia Britannica.* https://www.britannica.com/topic/cybercrime

Cybercrime. (2020). In *Merriam-Webster.* https://www.merriam-webster.com/dictionary/cybercrime

Cybercrime. (2020). In *Oxford Advanced Learner's Dictionary.*
https://www.oxfordlearnersdictionaries.com/definition/english/cybercrime

Cybercrime. (2020). In *The Chambers Dictionary.*
https://www.cybercrimechambers.com/blog-web-jacking-117.php

Dollard, J., Miller, N. E., Doob, L. W., Mowrer, O. H., & Sears, R. R. (1939). *Frustration and aggression*. New Haven, CT: Yale University Press.

Edwards, G. (2019). *Cybercrime investigators* (1ˢᵗ ed.). Hoboken, Wiley. ISBN-13: 978-1119596288

Elder, G. H., George, L. K., & Shanahan, M. J. (1996). Psychosocial stress over the life course. In Howard B. Kaplan (Ed.), *Psychosocial stress*. San Diego, CA: Academic Press.

Freilich, J. D., & Natarajan, M. (2009). Ronald Clarke. In K. Haywood, S. Maruna, & J. Mooney (Eds.), *Fifty key thinkers in criminology* (pp. 238-242). New York: Routledge.

Freilich, J. D., & Newman, G. R. (2016). Transforming piecemeal social engineering into "grand" crime prevention policy: Toward a new criminology of social control. *Journal of Criminal Law and Criminology, 105,* 203-232

Geen, R. G. (2001). *Human aggression*. Philadelphia, PA: Open University Press.

Gillespie, A. A. (2019). *Cybercrime: Key issues and debates*, London, Routledge. ISBN: 9781351010283

Graham, R. S., & Smith, S. K. (2019). *Cybercrime and digital deviance* (1ˢᵗ ed.). New York, Routledge. ISBN: 9780815376316

Hinduja, S., & Kooi, B. (2013). Curtailing cyber and information security vulnerabilities through situational crime prevention. *Security Journal, 26,* 383-402.

Hudak, H. C. (2019). *Cybercrime (Privacy in the digital age)*. North Star Editions. ISBN-13: 978-1644940815

Hufnagel, S., & Moiseienko, A. (2019). *Criminal networks and law enforcement: Global perspectives on illegal enterprise.* London, Routledge.

Hutchings, A. (2013). *Theory and crime: Does it compute?*. Australia: Griffith University.

International Monetary Fund (2020). *World economic outlook database.* https://www.imf.org/external/pubs/ft/weo/2019/02/weodata/index.aspx

Johansen, G. (2020). *Digital forensics and incident response: Incident response techniques and procedures to respond to modern cyber threats.* Packt Publishing.

Kim, P. (2018). *The hacker playbook 3: Practical guide to penetration testing.* Independently published.

Lagerspetz, K. M. J., Bjorkqvist, K., & Peltonen, T. (1988). Is indirect aggression typical of females? Gender differences in aggressiveness in 11 to 12 year old children. *Aggressive behavior, 14*(6), 403-414.

Lavorgna, A. (2020). *Cybercrimes: Critical issues in a global context.* Springer. ISBN-13: 978-1352009118

Leukfeldt, R., & Holt, T. J. (2019). *The human factor of cybercrime.* London, Routledge. ISBN-13: 978-1138624696

Littler, M., & Lee, B. (2020). *Digital extremisms: Readings in violence, radicalisation and extremism in the online space.* Cham, Springer Nature Switzerland AG. ISBN13: 9783030301378

Lusthaus, J. (2012). Trust in the world of cybercrime. *Global Crime, 13*(2), 71-94.

Malmuth, N. M, Addison, T., & Koss, M. (2000). Pornography and sexual aggression: Are
there reliable effects and can we understand them? *Annual Review of Sex Research, 11*,
26-91.

Marion, N. E., & Twede, J. (2020). *Cybercrime: An encyclopedia of digital crime.* Santa
Barbara, ABC-CLIO. ISBN-13: 978-1440857348

Marsh, B., & Melville, G. (2019). *Crime, justice and the media.* London, Routledge. ISBN:
9780429432194

Martellozzo, E., & Jane, E. A. (2017). *Cybercrime and its victims*. London, Routledge.

Mazerolle, P., Burton, V. S., Cullen, F. T., Evans, D., & Payne, G. L. (2000). Strain, anger, and
delinquency adaptations: Specifying general strain theory. *Journal of Criminal Justice,
28,* 89-101.

Merton, R. K. (1967). *On theoretical sociology.* Free Press.

Nassaji, H. (2015). Qualitative and descriptive research: Data type versus data analysis.
Language Teaching Research, 19(2), 129-132.

Newman, G. R. (1997). Introduction: Toward a theory of situational crime prevention. In G.
Newman, R. V. Clarke, & S. G. Shoham (Eds.), *Rational choice and situational crime
prevention* (pp. 1-23). Aldershot, U.K.: Ashgate Publishing.

Patchin, J. W., & Hinduja, S. (2011). Traditional and nontraditional bullying among youth: A
test of general strain theory. *Youth & Society, 43,* (2), 727-752.

Runions, K. C. (2013). Toward a conceptual model of motive and self-control in cyber-aggression: Rage,revenge, reward, and recreation. *Journal of Youth and Adolescence, 42,* 751-771.

Sangster, M. (2020). *No safe harbour: The inside truth about cybercrime and how to protect your business.* Vancouver, Page Two.

Schober, S. N., & Schober, C. W. (2019). *Cybersecurity is everybody's business: Solve the security puzzle for your small business and home.* ScottSchober.com Publishing.

Scott, J., & Marshall, G. (2009). *A dictionary of sociology.* (3rd ed.). Oxford University Press.

Steinberg, J. (2019). *Cybersecurity for dummies (For dummies computer/tech).* Hoboken, John Wiley & Sons. ISBN: 9781119560326

Tilley, N. (2004). Karl Popper: A philosopher for Ronald Clarke's situational crime prevention. *Israel Studies in Criminology, 8,* 39-56.

Troia, V. (2020). *Hunting cyber criminals: A hacker's guide to online Intelligence gathering tools and techniques.* Indianapolis, Wiley.

Willems, E. (2019). *Cyber danger: Understanding and guarding against cybercrime.* Springer.

Yar, M., & Steinmetz, K. F. (2019). *Cybercrime and society* (3rd ed.). SAGE Publications Ltd.

Zillmann, D. (1979). *Hostility and aggression.* Hillsdale, NJ: Lawrence Erlbaum Associates.

Additional Readings

1. Bandura, A. (2007). Reflections on an agentic theory of human behavior. *Tidsskrift for Norsk Norsk Psykologforening. 10,* 995-1004.

2. Bandura, A. (2007). Impeding ecological sustainability through selective moral disengagement. *The Int'l. Journal of Innovation and Sustainable Development, 2,* 8-35.

3. Cloward, R., & Ohlin, L. (2013). *Delinquency and opportunity: A study of delinquent gangs.* Routledge.

4. Cornish, D. B., & Clarke, R. V. (Eds.). (2014). *The reasoning criminal: Rational choice perspectives on offending.* NJ: Transaction Publishers.

5. Downes, D. M., & Rock, P. (2011). *Understanding deviance: A guide to the sociology of crime and rule-breaking.* Oxford, UK: Oxford University Press.

6. Hagan, F. E. (2012). *Introduction to criminology: Theories, methods, and criminal behavior.* Los Angeles, CA: Sage.

7. Hirschi, T. (1969). *Causes of delinquency.* Berkeley: University of California Press.

8. Hutchings, A. (2013). *Theory and crime: Does it compute?.* Australia: Griffith University.

9. Isajiw, W. W. (2013). *Causation and functionalism in sociology.* Routledge.

10. Jordan, T., & Taylor, P. (1998). A sociology of hackers. *The Sociological Review, 46*(4), 757-780.

Key Terms

1. **Anonymity:** The condition of being unknown.

2. **Cybercrime:** The use of a computer to commit a crime.

3. **Cyberstalking:** The use of Information and Communication Technology to frighten or harass an individual or group.

4. **Cyberworld:** The world of inter-computer communication.

5. **Hacking:** To gain unauthorized access to data in a system or computer.

Chapter 2: Contemporaneous Approach to Cybercrime Varieties and Skills

Abstract

Several thousand organized groups as well as gangs and are dedicated to cybercrime. The rewards for even simple cybercrime can be immense for what is relatively little effort. The advancement of technology will certainly lead to a transformation of cybercrime which is why, some prefer to think of cybercrime as an ever changing set of behavior. Where, technology could be programmed to be beneficial it could equally programmed to be harmful. It is sometime tempting to downplay cybercrime, painting it always being the action of a lone individual, but while this is true of some crimes, the reality of cybercrime as a whole is very different. In the contemporary era, several thousand groups are dedicated to cybercrime because of the rewards attached to it. Cybercrime's pace globally is on a high rise. It is an offense that is even harder to identify and resolve as compared to traditional crimes in the international context. Cybercrime cells all around the world receives thousands of complaints on a daily basis. Cyber criminals are honing their skills, while consumers remain unconcerned. Cyber criminals are innovative, organized, and far sophisticated. They employ their tools effectively, working harder, and focused to uncover new vulnerabilities as well as escape detection. The ICTs are opening a whole new world of opportunities for criminals and the risk remains largely unknown.

Keywords: *cybercrime, hacking, malware, pharming, phishing, skills, spyware*

Introduction

Cybercrime has so advanced that it was reported in August 2018 during the Black Hat and Def Con Hacking Conference that, it was possible to even hack patients' vital signs, pacemaker, and insulin pumps in real time (Smith, 2018). Symantec, one of the leading software firms that operates antivirus and firewall packages, stated in their 'Internet Security Threat Report 2011' (published in 2012) that there had been an 81% increase in malicious attacks that they had identified, with an estimate of attacks being placed over 5.5 billion.

A Barkly sponsored survey of 660 IT companies and professionals by Ponemon Institute, USA (2018) 'State of Endpoint Security Risk' has revealed that 64% of organizations experienced successful endpoint attacks. This survey has also revealed zero-day and fileless attacks that cost millions to organizations, i.e. costs doubling for Small and Medium-sized Businesses (SMBs). Findings by a research organization, Comparitech, Mr. Paul Bischoff (2018) claims that stock prices are adversely effected by data breaches. In case of a data breach, it can lead to around 0.5 percent decrease in a firm's overall share in market.

At the very least, it demonstrates the fact that cybercrime attacks are an almost routine form of criminality and most internet users are likely to face an attack on a daily basis, but perhaps do not realize this because they rely on automatic protection systems.

A new study, conducted by Bromium and Dr. Michael McGuire, senior lecturer in criminology at the University of Surrey in England, presented at the RSA Conference 2018 in San Francisco has found that the cybercrime economy has grown to $1.5 trillion dollars annually. Cybersecurity Ventures is world's renowned research company with regards to global cyber economy as well as cyber security. In their official annual Cybercrime Report 2017 they predicted that cybercrime will cost the world around $6 trillion annually by 2021.

Cybercrime can be defined in multiple ways; in the broadest sense, any offense involving a computer system may be included in this category. Few definitions encompassing the subject matter are cited.

According to Merriam-Webster (2020), "Criminal activity (such as fraud, theft, or distribution of child pornography) committed using a computer especially to illegally access, transmit, or manipulate data". While, in accordance with Oxford Advanced Learner's Dictionary (2020), "Crime that is committed using the internet, for example by stealing somebody's personal or bank details or by infecting their computer with a virus".

"Cybercrime is a crime committed by means of computers or the internet" (Collins English Dictionary, 2020). While according to The Chambers Dictionary (2020), "Criminal activity or a crime that involves the internet, a computer system, or computer technology".

Encyclopedia Britannica (2020) states, "Cybercrime, the use of a computer as an instrument to further illegal ends, such as committing fraud, trafficking in child pornography and intellectual property, stealing identities, or violating privacy. Cybercrime, especially through the Internet, has grown in importance as the computer has".

Focus of the Research

This research focuses on 11 varieties and nine skill levels involved in cybercrime. Cybercrime statistics along with top 10 countries facing cybercrime are also highlighted. Cybercrime being a multifaceted problem requires a comprehensive approach as the respective subject matter is far more complex to comprehend.

Objectives

1. To analyze the varieties of cybercrime.

2. To describe the skills involved in cybercrime.

3. To elaborate cybercrime statistics.

Research Methodology

This research was formed by a systematic review method (Komba & Lwoga, 2020). In this method, the research objectives are determined and an extensive literature review is made on the subject. The research findings obtained are classified according to the content of the subject (Petticrew & Roberts, 2006). Classified information is included in the study by organizing it as headings (Pawson et al., 2005). The flow of the study is formed by evaluating classified information and titles (Rahi, 2017). Thus, integrity is ensured by evaluating the researched subject with its contents (Victor, 2008).

As a result, this method was adopted and these procedures were followed respectively. The information and data obtained from the literature review related to the research objectives were coded. The coded information was combined under the related topics. After classification and combining, the topics were sorted according to their level of relationship.

Varieties and Skills of Cybercrime

Cybercrime involves various skills and varies greatly, but enlisted aspects have been much stressed upon in the work of scholars like, Bancroft (2019); Johansen (2020); Leukfeldt and Holt (2019); Steinberg (2019); and Troia (2020).

1. Hacking of Computers

Hacking is considered to be improperly accessing to a computer, that one does not have authority to, and this usage could be considered as an unlawful access. However, the internet has revolutionized the way hacking takes place in the contemporary era (Hutchings, 2013). The internet is a network of connections. Therefore, no matter where a computer is hosted, the internet can exploit these respective connections and gain access to them virtually. There is a common belief that it is one of the most ominous form of cybercrime (Moore, 2005).

'Hacker' was once a term of pride applied to those that had superior computer skills. It was simply the demonstration of programming skills (Sandwell, 2010). While, the term 'Cracker' has also been used in place of hacker, but the respective term did not really captured the public's attention. Hacking is comparatively more common with regards to government bodies as well as corporate entities. Majority of hacking is directed towards government and corporations rather than individuals (Beaver, 2017).

There are also other types of hackers distinguished by 'hats' and commonly there exists three 'hats':

    i.   **White hat:** The usage of hacking techniques to test respective security measures.

    ii.   **Black hat:** An attempt of a malicious hacking not only to look around, but to steal or damage website, servers, or files.

    iii.   **Grey hat:** It has the least clear definition, but is considered to be someone who is somewhere between the above-cited categories.

Hacking is a complex phenomenon as it involves humans. Therefore, it is believed that a more rationalistic approach regarding hacker's behavior is required. It can be categories as enlisted:

    i.   **Novice:** A person new to hacking who tends to rely on the programs of others to assist in the hacking.

ii. **Cyber Punk:** A person more technologically astute than the novice and who tends to undertake low-level malicious acts.

iii. **Internas:** A disgruntled employee or ex-employee who uses the authorization he has been given to maliciously damage or leak content.

iv. **Petty Thieves:** A person who uses his hacking skills not for notoriety and gain access to a damage site, etc., but to rather steal money.

v. **Virus Writer:** An individual or a group that writes viruses.

vi. **Old Guard Hacker:** A person who does not have any overtly malicious intentions and is hacking to show skill or to look for information.

vii. **Professional Criminals:** A person who belongs to a professional and organized gang and who uses hacking to make significant financial gains.

viii. **Information Warriors:** A person who uses hacking to launch attacks on command and control activities of a state.

ix. **Political Activist:** A person who uses hacking for political purposes.

2. Denial of Service Attacks (DoS)

As hacking was solely about the infiltration of a computer. It is also being increasingly used to undertake Distributed Denial of Services (DDoS) and Denial of Services (DoS) attacks (Moore, 2005). In a DoS attack websites or servers are targeted via overloading it, i.e., to make it as unusable. Criminal perpetrators of DoS attacks often target sites or services hosted on high-profile web servers such as banks or credit card payment gateways. Revenge, blackmail, and activism can motivate these attacks.

Websites as well as servers can only manage a specific limit of traffic. It is possible to overwhelm a server and either slow it down or cause it to crash. For example, a popular commerce site is offering huge sales and advertise it and said that site 'crashes' because too many people are trying to buy at the same time, a DoS attack works on the same principle.

3. Distributed Denial of Services Attacks (DDoS)

A distributed denial-of-service (DDoS) attack is a malicious attempt to disrupt normal traffic of a targeted server, service or network by overwhelming the target or its surrounding infrastructure with a flood of Internet traffic. A DDoS operates in the same way as DoS attack, but it involves multiple computers.

Sometimes this will be concentrated effort of people who will communicate through peer-to-peer networks which allows an attack to be made, and for the attack to be varied as the targeted computer tries to evade the attack.In it 'zombies' or 'bots' are used mostly (Beaver, 2017).

This is where a hacked computer is 'taken over' by the hackers and instructions passed to the computer. With multiple 'bots' it means that the attack can take place from different computers and IP addresses making it more difficult for the operator of the attacked server to respond to the attack, since as they block one IP address another can simply take over.

4. Malware

The second principal attack that takes place against technology is that of malware. i.e., software that targets computers for malicious purposes (Dunham, 2009). For example virus is a type of malware. There are three principal categories:

i.   **Virus:** It is a self-replication program that seeks to spread itself by attaching itself either to a particular file or storage medium. When it detects that it has been placed into a new device, it will embed itself there. Sometimes, the virus is programmed to increase the likelihood of someone opening it.

ii. **Worm:** It is similar to a virus because they work on self-replication, but are also autonomous. A virus would attach itself to a file or a storage device and be spread in that way. While, a worm exploits the connectivity of the internet.

iii. **Trojan:** It is a type of malware that is often disguised as legitimate software. Trojans can be employed by hackers trying to gain access to users' systems. Users are typically tricked by some form of social engineering into loading and executing trojans on their systems. A trojan permits a person to have remote access to the computer and therefore they could. However, they can take over the functions of the computer. This could include for example, the webcam.

5. Spyware

Spyware differs from viruses, worms and trojans, because its focus is on the invasion of privacy rather than causing damage to the system or direct stealing of financial information (Smith, 2018). The use of key loggers, pop-ups, and website monitoring can amount to spyware, but where it facilitates remote access this could equally be classified as a trojan.

While, viruses, worms, and trojans are likely to be developed by individuals, spyware could arise from legitimate companies. Google, Microsoft, and Apple have all been accused at one time of using spyware. The use of spyware, including tracking cookies, can be a very big business with companies prepare to pay a lot of money for information about how the user act (Beaver, 2017).

6. Offense Relating to Data

However, directly related to this are offenses relating to data There are four issues particularly, although they do overlap to an extent (Urbas & Choo, 2008).

i. Destroying data

ii.   Inappropriate access to data

iii. Unlawful disclosure of data

iv.   Interception of data

7. Destroying, Disclosing, and Accessing Data

There are two ways in which the destruction, access, or disclosure of data can occur. The first is where an individual or group gains unlawful access to a computer system and either destroy, access, or discloses the data that they have found or, in respect of destroying data, infects a computer with malware. The second is where someone who is authorized to access the computer then subsequently destroy or disclose data without authority (Smith, 2018).

8. Misconduct in a Public Office

Another offense that is the common law offense is the misconduct in public office. It may include, intentionally misconduct or neglect to perform duty. The use of authority to an extent to abuse the public's trust regarding the office holder. It can be also without justification or a reasonable excuse (Beaver, 2017).

9. Phishing

Anyone using an email account could possibly receive a phishing email, and it can happen it different ways. For example, asking an individual to confirm their credentials, so the phisher can access confidential information or send spam from the account. It indeed is a clever technique, because it will fool an individual easily. The respective individual believes that he is calling his bank and the email is correct. Therefore, he is more prepared to confirm his bank details (Sandwell, 2010).

10. Pharming

It is where a fake website is created instead of fake email. An individual believes that he is trying to reach an original website, but is actually diverted to a rogue website. This would be achieved by polluting the technical process of a computer, so that the Domain Name System (DNS) which allows a user to navigate to a particular site will take the user to a fake website. The most usual way of doing this is through the provision of malware (Urbas & Choo, 2008).

The major difficulty with farming is that the user will probably not know that the site they are accessing is not legitimate, and will feel safe because they took precautions by. For example, entering the website for online banking.

Another popular way of farming is to rely on what is popularly known as 'fat finger' syndrome. The second form of phishing relies on this phenomenon. The person operating the scam will create a duplicate site, but one which contain a spelling mistake (example, meirto.com instead of merito.com), and there are only few people who actually see their Uniform Resource Locator (URL) or in simple words, the 'web address' displayed in internet browser. If an individual types an address for a site, and a site appears that look like the one that he wished to access, then most people will probably trust that the website is correct and do not check its URL.

11. Hate and Harm

The issue of hate is referred to as 'hate speech', which is a form of expression, i.e., odious in its very nature, and people are targeted on the basis of their religion, color, race, physical characteristics - including disability, as well as sexuality (Ogilvie, 2000).

While, 'harm' and 'self-harm' websites encourage actions of a person to an extent that they could cause harm to others as well as themselves. This include suicide websites, cutting websites, and those related to eating disorders (Yar, 2013).

Both 'hate speech' and 'harm' websites are linked by the fact that they relate to content and non-physical contact. These websites possess offensive and unpleasant content that is undoubtedly from a moral perspective unacceptable and unhealthy.

Cybercrime Statistics

According to Alvarez Technology Group (2018); Devon Milkovich (2018); and Patrick Nohe (2018) these are few of the most alarming cybercrime statistics:

1. 95% of breached records came from only three industries worldwide, government, retail, and technology.

2. There is a hacker attack every 39 seconds in US alone according to the study conducted by the Clark School at the University of Maryland, USA.

3. 43% of cyber attacks target small business. 64% of companies have experienced web-based attacks. 62% experienced phishing & social engineering attacks. 59% of companies experienced malicious code and botnets and 51% experienced denial of service attacks.

4. The average cost of a data breach in 2020 will exceed $150 million according to Juniper Research data.

5. Since 2013 there are 3,809,448 records stolen from breaches every day.

6. According to the Q2 2018 Threat Report, Nexusguard's quarterly report, the average distributed denial-of-service (DDoS) attack grew to more than 26Gbps, increasing in size by 500%.

7. Approximately $6 trillion is expected to be spent globally on cyber security by 2021.

8. Unfilled cyber security jobs worldwide will reach $3.5 million by 2021.

9. By 2020 there will be roughly 200 billion connected devices, which means more exposure to cybercrime.

10. 95% of cyber security breaches are due to human error.

11. Only 38% of global organizations claim they are prepared to handle a sophisticated cyber attack.

12. Total cost for cybercrime committed globally has added up to over $1 trillion dollars in 2018.

Top 10 Countries Facing Cybercrime

According to Sumo3000 (2018), following are the top ten countries that are facing cybercrime. These 10 countries face around 63% of the total cybercrime committed across the globe.

1. USA (23%)

2. China (9%)

3. Germany (6%)

4. Britain (5%)

5. Brazil (4%)

6. Spain (4%)

7. Italy (3%)

8. France (3%)

9. Turkey (3%)

10. Poland (3%)

Solutions and Recommendations

1. Awareness could be spread with regards to cybercrime. It can be done via engaging community as well as CBOs, NGOs, INGOs, and cyber vigilantism.

2. Victims of cybercrime are large in number, there should be easy access of the victims where they can complain regarding e-offenses.

3. The respective legal departments should be equipped with the latest investigating technologies.

4. Terminate online sessions completely.

5. Use your own computer and when using a public computer avoid online transactions if possible.

6. Use security programs and protect your passwords.

7. Use privacy settings to prevent personal information being broadcast via social networking.

8. Clear all your history after logging off your account.

9. Update your software package regularly.

10. Do not open any links in emails from strangers.

11. Encryption of file and regular backups of significant data.

12. Limiting the administrative powers of all accounts in case of a shared devices.

13. Unknown Wi-Fi networks and Bluetooth connections should be avoided.

14. Visiting only trustworthy websites.

15. E-transactions must be entered via websites that are authentic, and data should not be saved on online servers.

Future Research Directions

Significant areas for conducting future research encompassing cybercrime via engaging qualitative, qualitative, or eclectic approach can be:

1. Computer-focused as well as computer-assisted crimes

2. Criminal psychology

3. Cyberterrorism

4. Cyber security

5. Ethical hacking

6. Hacktivism

7. Incident response planning

8. Malware

9. Perceived and actual risks in cyberworld

10. Vulnerabilities in computing

Conclusion

It is clearly evident that as people become more dependent on technology, they become easier targets of cybercrime as it also could evolve to bring about new problems. As cybercrime is a multifaceted problem, therefore, a multidimensional approach is required to understand the subject matter of the respective issue. Nations worldwide are facing the hazards of cybercrime, because of numerous causes, poor technology, lack of cooperation with international law enforcing agencies, and absence as well as incapacity of legislation to financial constraints. Thus, solutions to the problems posed must be addressed by international law, necessitating the adoption of adequate international legal instruments. The dire need of ICT applications in privatized as well as government sector is today's prerequisite, because utilization of these applications have enhanced operational effectiveness. On the contrary, intemperate usage of computer networks as well as its applications has amplified issues encompassing the phenomenon of cybercrime. Comprehensive cyber laws in an international context are a dire need of time. Furthermore, cyber laws have been developed in almost every developing as well as developed country, but their implementation is comparatively weak.

References

Alvarez Technology Group (2018). *2018 top cybercrime facts and why you should care.*

https://www.alvareztg.com/2018-cybercrime-statistics-reference- material/

Bancroft, A. (2019). *The darknet and smarter crime: Methods for Investigating criminal entrepreneurs and the illicit drug economy (Palgrave studies in cybercrime and cybersecurity).* Cham, Palgrave Macmillan. ISBN-13: 978-3030265113

Beaver, K. (2017). *Hacking for dummies* (5th ed). ISBN-13: 978-1119154686

Bischoff, P. (2018, September 6). *Analysis: How data breaches affect stock market share prices.*

https://www.comparitech.com/blog/information-security/data-breach- share-price-2018/

Black Hat and Def Con Hacking Conference. (August - 2018).

https://www.blackhat.com/us-18/defcon.html

Bromium, & McGuire, M. (2018, April). *RSA Conference 2018.* San Francisco, USA.

https://www.rsaconference.com/events/us18

Cybercrime. (2020). In *Collins English Dictionary.*

https://www.collinsdictionary.com/dictionary/english/cybercrime

Cybercrime. (2020). In *Encyclopedia Britannica.* https://www.britannica.com/topic/cybercrime

Cybercrime. (2020). In *Merriam-Webster.* https://www.merriam-webster.com/dictionary/cybercrime

Cybercrime. (2020). In *Oxford Advanced Learner's Dictionary.*

https://www.oxfordlearnersdictionaries.com/definition/english/cybercrime

Cybercrime. (2020). In *The Chambers Dictionary.*

https://www.cybercrimechambers.com/blog-web-jacking-117.php

Cybersecurity Ventures. Cybercrime Report, 2017.

https://cybersecurityventures.com/hackerpocalypse-cybercrime-report-2016/

Dunham, K. (2009). *Mobile malware attacks and defense.* MA: Syngress Publishing.

Hutchings, A. (2013). *Theory and crime: Does it compute?.* Australia: Griffith University.

Johansen, G. (2020). *Digital forensics and incident response: Incident response techniques and procedures to respond to modern cyber threats.* Birmingham, Packt Publishing.

ISBN-13: 978-1838649005

Komba, M. M., & Lwoga, E. T. (2020). *Systematic review as a research method in library and information science.* DOI: 10.4018/978-1-7998-1471-9.ch005.

Leukfeldt, R., & Holt, T. J. (2019). *The human factor of cybercrime.* London, Routledge.

Milkovich, D. (2018, December 3). *13 alarming cyber security facts and stats.*

https://www.cybintsolutions.com/cyber-security-facts-stats/

Moore, R. (2005). Cybercrime: Investigating high technology computer crime. NY: Matthew Bender & Company. ISBN 1-59345-303-5.

Nohe, P. (2018, September 27). *Re-hashed: 2018 cybercrime statistics: A closer look at the web of profit".* https://www.thesslstore.com/blog/2018-cybercrime-statistics/

Ogilvie, E. (2000). Cyberstalking. *Trends and Issues in Crime and Criminal Justice,* 166.

Pawson, R., Greenhalgh, T., Harvey, G, & Walshe, K. (2005). Realist review - A new method of systematic review designed for complex policy interventions. *Journal of Health Services Research & Policy, 10*(1), 21-34.

Petticrew, M., & Roberts, H. (2006). *Systematic reviews in the social sciences: A practical guide.* DOI: 10.1002/9780470754887

Ponemon Institute. (2018). *State of Endpoint Security Risk.*

    https://www.businesswire.com/news/home/20181016005758/en/Study-Reveals64-

    Organizations-Experienced-Successful-Endpoint

Rahi, S. (2017). Research design and methods: A systematic review of research paradigms,

    sampling issues and instruments development. *International Journal of Economics &*

    Management Sciences, (6). DOI: 10.4172/2162-6359.1000403.

Sandwell, B. (2010). On the globalisation of crime: The internet and new criminality. In Y.

    Jewkes & M. Yar, *Handbook of internet crime* (pp. 38-66). England: Willan Publishing.

Smith. (2018). *Hacking pacemakers, insulin pumps and patients' vital signs in real time.*

    https://www.csoonline.com/article/3296633/security/hacking-pacemakers-insulin-pumps-an

    d-patients-vital-signs-in-real-time.html

Steinberg, J. (2019). *Cybersecurity for dummies (For dummies computer/tech).*Hoboken, John

    Wiley & Sons. ISBN: 9781119560326

Summo3000 (2018). *Top 20 countries found to have the most cybercrime.*

    https://www.enigmasoftware.com/top-20-countries-the-most-cybercrime/

Symantec White Paper - Turning the Tables on Malware. (2012).

    https://www.symantec.com/content/en/us/enterprise/white_papers/b-turning_the_ tab

    les_on_malware_WP_21155056.en-us.pdf

Troia, V. (2020). *Hunting cyber criminals: A hacker's guide to online Intelligence gathering*

    tools and techniques. Indianapolis, Wiley. ISBN-13: 978-1119540922

Urbas, G., & Choo, K. R. (2008). *Resource materials on technology-enabled crime.* Canberra,

    Australia: Australian Institute of Criminology. ISBN: 9781921185700.

Victor, L. (2008). Systematic reviewing in the social sciences: Outcomes and explanation .
Enquire 1(1), 32-46.

Yar, M. (2013). *Cybercrime and society.* London: Sage Publishing Ltd.

Additional Readings

1. Alazab, M., & Broadhurst, R. (2014). *Spam and criminal activity. Trends and issues.* Australia: Australian Institute of Criminology.

2. Bandura, A. (2007). Reflections on an agentic theory of human behavior. *Tidsskrift for Norsk Norsk Psykologforening. 10,* 995-1004.

3. Bandura, A. (2007). Impeding ecological sustainability through selective moral disengagement. *The International Journal of Innovation and Sustainable Development, 2,* 8-35.

4. Brenner, S. W. (2014). *Cyberthreats and the decline of the nation-state.* NY: Routledge.

5. Broadhurst, R., & Choo, K. K. R. (2011). *Cybercrime and online safety in cyberspace.* Routledge Handbook of Criminology.

6. Cloward, R., & Ohlin, L. (2013). *Delinquency and opportunity: A study of delinquent gangs.* Routledge.

7. Cornish, D. B., & Clarke, R. V. (Eds.). (2014). *The reasoning criminal: Rational choice perspectives on offending.* NJ: Transaction Publishers.

8. Downes, D. M., & Rock, P. (2011). *Understanding deviance: A guide to the sociology of crime and rule-breaking.* Oxford, UK: Oxford University Press.

9. Ekblom, P. (2014). Designing products against crime. In *Encyclopedia of Criminology and Criminal Justice* (pp. 948-957). NY: Springer.

10. Glenny, M. (2012). *DarkMarket: How hackers became the new media.* NY: Vintage Books.

11. Hagan, F. E. (2012). *Introduction to criminology: Theories, methods, and criminal behavior.* Los Angeles, CA: Sage.

12. Hirschi, T. (1969). *Causes of delinquency.* Berkeley: University of California Press.

13. Hutchings, A. (2013). *Theory and crime: Does it compute?.* Australia: Griffith University.

14. Isajiw, W. W. (2013). *Causation and functionalism in sociology.* NY: Routledge.

15. Jordan, T., & Taylor, P. (1998). A sociology of hackers. *The Sociological Review, 46*(4), 757-780.

16. Maurushat, A. (2013). Discovery and dissemination of discovering security vulnerabilities. In *Disclosure of Security Vulnerabilities* (pp. 21-33). London: Springer.

17. McGuire, M. (2012). *Organised crime in the digital age.* London: John Grieve Centre for Policing and Security.

18. Sternberg, J. (2012). *Misbehavior in cyber places: The regulation of online conduct in virtual communities on the internet.* MD: Rowman & Littlefield.

19. Webber, C. (2014). *Hackers and cybercrime. Shades of deviance: A primer on crime, deviance and social harm.* London: Routledge.

20. Zhang, X., Tsang, A., Yue, W. T., & Chau, M. (2015). The classification of hackers by knowledge exchange behaviors. *Information Systems Frontiers,* 1-13.

Key Terms

1. **Cybercrime:** The use of a computer to commit a crime.

2. **Denial of Service attack:** It is an attack to shut down a machine or network, making it inaccessible to its intended users.

3. **Distributed Denial of Service attack:** It is a malicious attempt to disrupt normal traffic, to make it impossible for a service to be delivered.

4. **Malware:** Any file or program that is harmful to a computer user as well as sensitive information.

5. **Pharming:** It is a cyber attack that intends to redirect a website's traffic to a fake site.

6. **Phishing:** It is a fraudulent attempt to obtain sensitive information.

7. **Spyware:** An unwanted software that infiltrates any computing device, stealing data.

Chapter 3: Predicaments Encompassing Pakistan's Cybercrime Victimization

Abstract

Research studies into cybercrime with regards to the Pakistani context are nominal, as the field is relatively new. Pakistani has a perfect ecosystem regarding cybercrime, as the internet is widely available. The use of social media in Pakistan is increasing exponentially. Adults who carry out online transactions and store important data on their computers are at a high risk of financial theft and hacking in Pakistan. Laws regarding cybercrime exist in Pakistan, but are rarely enforced. The respective culprits usually go largely unpunished in Pakistan. The National Assembly of Pakistan passed the Electronic Crime Bill 2016 after making various amendments to it. Even this bill faced severe opposition in Pakistan. This study asses and analyze cybercrime's current state in the Pakistani context.

Keywords: *cybercrime, cyberterrorism, cyber world, cyber security, dilemma, hacking, Pakistan, victims*

Introduction

Anusha Rahman Khan - Minister of State for Information Technology and Telecommunication of Pakistan and member of the committee for development of 'Prevention of Electronic Crimes Act, 2016' (PECA) admitted in a summarized note that, Pakistan has no such laws before to deal comprehensively with cybercrime. She also admitted that, criminal justice legal framework is ill equipped as well as inadequate and to resolve the respective threats of the cyber age. In Pakistan, National Response Centre for Cyber Crime (NR3C) was established in 2007.

It is sometime tempting to downplay cybercrime, painting it always being the action of a lone individual, but while this is true of some crimes, the reality of cybercrime as a whole is very different (Benson & McAlaney, 2019; Johansen, 2020; Troia, 2020; Yar & Steinmetz, 2019). In contemporary era, several thousand groups are dedicated to cybercrime because of the rewards attached to it (Austin, 2020; Gillespie, 2019; Leukfeldt & Holt, 2019). It is clearly evident that as people become more dependent on technology, they become easier targets of cybercrime (Hudak, 2019; Martellozzo & Jane, 2017; Steinberg, 2019), as it also could evolve to bring about new problems (Hufnagel & Moiseienko, 2019; Marion & Twede, 2020). It is also important to realize to what extent it is understood by people that either they are really a victim or can be the victim of a cybercrime (Abaimov & Martellini, 2020; Marsh & Melville, 2019).

It is important to realize to what extent cybercrime is understood by people that either they are really a victim or can be the victim of a cybercrime (Azevedo, 2019; Carlson, 2019; Steinberg, 2019). For example, the sending of emails trying to influence people to enter their bank detail is illegal, but almost every one with an email address will have received an email asking them to confirm their bank details (Bancroft, 2019; Bandler & Merzon, 2020).Another problem is the issue in identifying victims of cybercrime are those situations where people do not know that they have been victimized (Edwards 2019; Graham & Smith, 2019; Hutchings, 2013; Sangster, 2020). Most users of the computer will be aware of the need to install firewall and antivirus software (Littler & Lee, 2020; Schober & Schober; 2019). It is often rare for someone to be told that the program has stopped a virus or potential hack (Kim, 2018; Lavorgna, 2020; Willems, 2019).

"Cybercrime is a crime committed by means of computers or the internet" (Collins English Dictionary, 2020). While according to The Chambers Dictionary (2020), "Criminal activity or a crime that involves the internet, a computer system, or computer technology".

Encyclopedia Britannica (2020) states, "Cybercrime, the use of a computer as an instrument to further illegal ends, such as committing fraud, trafficking in child pornography and intellectual property, stealing identities, or violating privacy. Cybercrime, especially through the Internet, has grown in importance as the computer has".

According to Merriam-Webster (2020), "Criminal activity (such as fraud, theft, or distribution of child pornography) committed using a computer especially to illegally access, transmit, or manipulate data". While, in accordance with Oxford Advanced Learner's Dictionary (2020), "Crime that is committed using the internet, for example by stealing somebody's personal or bank details or by infecting their computer with a virus".

This research includes case studies, involving violations of authenticity, confidentiality, as well as human integrity. This is often elaborated through different newspapers as well as TV channels of Pakistan. Their authenticity is checked through multiple reliable sources, like press release or law enforcement agencies of Pakistan, namely the Federal Investigation Agency,

National Database and Registration Authority, Provincial Police Department, etc. related to computer-crime and cybercrime division, as well as through multiple relevant and authentic websites.

This involves six cases regarding cybercrime, the outcome of the case, and information based on evidence from the case, as well as the background of criminals. Different case studies provide a wide spectrum of perspectives into what types of cybercrime are getting common, and how the virtual world or cyber space are the area which needs utmost attention to contain and control cyber criminals in the Pakistani context.

Focus of the Research

This research asses and analyze cybercrime's current state in the Pakistani context. The incidents with victim's name changed are documented in this research. The following case studies were chosen because these are the most prominent cases that made headlines and are still in debate across the country. The purpose of this research is to assist legislators, corporate executives, law enforcement agencies, academicians, criminal justice officials, IT managers, as well as other professionals.

Research Methodology

This study focuses on cybercrime victimization in Pakistan. To this end, qualitative research methodology by using purposive sampling was adopted and six case studies were taken. That is the very reason, it is explanatory in its very nature.

Case Study 1 - ATM Fraud

A sudden overpowering fright spread among the people in Pakistan, when the news was broken regarding Automated Teller Machine (ATM) skimming fraud. The culprits collected information, like ATM card number and PIN code through the installation of skimming devices in ATM machines throughout Pakistan, especially Karachi. Criminals used the personal information for the withdrawal of cash in China and few other countries (Geo News, 2017).

Federal Investigation Agency (FIA) spoke about the matter and confirmed the theft of data and money of around 579 ATM cards users in December 2017. Criminals installed the skimming devices along with hidden cameras in ATMs. Account holders who were unaware of this theft were informed by their respective banks, the agency shared (Geo News, 2017).

Habib Bank Pvt. Ltd., one of the targeted bank also confirmed the theft and installation of skimming devices on four of its ATMs. Criminals installed three devices in Islamabad on different place and one in Karachi. The investigation has been started by FIA under the Prevention of Electronic Crimes Act. The involvement of transnational criminals belong to China has been identified during the investigation. The matter has been discussed on diplomatic level between Pakistan and Chinese officials. The details and evidence of the fraud has been shared by FIA with respective Chinese authorities (Geo News, 2017).

Placing of skimming devices need skills as well as expertise. It is usually used to gather the personal information of debit card user that includes debit card number and personal identification number (PIN). Criminals placed the fraudulent card reading devices which looks same as original on ATMs along with the keypad and a hidden camera which provides them the detailed log.

The offenders used to install the card reader on ATMs, so that the card information can be recorded and the use of camera was helping them to note down the PIN code type by the customers for withdrawing the cash. After recording the activities for few days, they reconciled the data and withdrew the money from other countries. Devices were placed in crowded shopping centres in city, like Karachi.

It was also revealed during the investigation that fraudster made other ATMs dysfunctional on the arena, so that more people used the tempered one. Which ultimately provided them with the maximum number of people's ATM cards information. This sort of cybercrime is not new of its type. According to Group-IB report, cyber criminals had earned more than £10.5 million by hacking the ATM cards information through out the world. It is estimated that offenders have already withdrawn around $2.6 from other parts of the world by this fraudulent use of technology (Cuthbertson, 2018).

The sales of the respective ATM cards and credit cards takes place mostly on the dark web. According to Group-IB findings, its rare to find the sales of ATM card on the dark web from a country like Pakistan. That is why, this is the only reported sales of cards in last six months (Cuthbertson, 2018). In an exclusive TV interview to Dawn News, Mr. Shoaib commented that bank should take the responsibility of this scam. They should have preventive measures to make sure the security of their customers data. The hackers have defrauded a huge amount from card holders accounts. He further said that, this event is an indication for banks to not only upgrade their IT security infrastructure, but to also go beyond strategically to ensure the prevention from future attacks (Zaidi, 2015).

Although, the State Bank of Pakistan has taken the notice and advised all banks to review their security polices to prevent future thefts. It denied about its operations being effected by any of the cyber attack. It is reported that in response to this scam, around six banks have debarred the international use of debit cards temporarily. This news is further endorsed by the chief spokesperson for the State Bank of Pakistan, Mr. Abid Qamar, as he stated that, "It has come to their notice that few banks have suspended the use of cards all over the world except Pakistan" (Geo News, 2017).

Case Study 2 - Hacking Government Websites

Pakistan is also among the effected countries of cyber attacks. Multiple websites have been targeted by black hat hackers. Even an army operated site was attacked, called DDoS attack by the international hackers, as a demo during a live interview to a radio channel. The group of hackers known as, New World Hackers, internationally attacked Pakistan's Frontier Constabulary website on January 10, 2016, while live interview on the Anon UK Radio was in process. It happened just few days after the wave of continuous attacks on government official site (Cuthbertson, 2016).

It is estimated that they almost attacked 60% of the government's official websites. In an statement by the hackers group New world Hackers told that it was not the direct attack from them, but they facilitated Indian hackers, as they were asked to support. The group operates independently, and still takes part in certain operations.

Most of the cyber attacks on Pakistani websites are initiated from India, and it is supposed that it was in response to Pathankot Air Force Base incident, a city in the Punjab state of India, on January 2-5, 2016, where, the death of 14 people was reported. The group further explained that Indians don't attack Pakistani websites for fun, but they take it as a war. The New World Hackers said that they upgraded the capabilities of the Indian hackers worldwide.

Case Study 3 - Illegal Online Drugs

Four members of a narcotics supply gang operating in Defence Housing Authority (DHA) and Clifton, Karachi were arrested in raids carried out by the District South Police (Karachi region) on September 18, 2017 (Perwaiz, 2017). The drug dealers used social media applications, including WhatsApp and Facebook for their transactions and their customer-base was largely comprised of youngsters from high-income localities, said Mr. Javed Akbar Riaz, the Senior Superintendent of Police for District South (Karachi) who supervised the raids.

The officer said teams had been tasked with the investigation after multiple complaints and reports were received regarding the gang's activities in Karachi. The investigators soon found out about the gang's use of Facebook and WhatsApp for communication with customers. Posing as potential buyers, the cops then approached the dealers on the social media platforms and tracked their location.

The team encountered resistance from the suspects, but eventually managed to apprehend two men identified as Ahsan Abbas alias Bilal Shaikh and Taha Kamil and seized a sizeable quantity of hashish. Interrogation revealed that Ahsan was heading the entire operation and the gang consisted in total of eight members.

Acting on information gleaned from the suspects, the police carried out another raid in DHA in which two more gang members, Ashraf Yaseen and Tabassum Hashim, were arrested with more narcotics. As per SSP Akbar Riaz, the gang's modus operandi was based on establishing friendly associations with susceptible youngsters. They (the gang members) would frequent parties and other social gatherings to befriend people. At first, they would offer drugs such as ice, cocaine, and hashish for free. They would wait for the person to develop a dependence on the substance and became a habitual user and then start extorting large sums of money from him or her.

He confirmed the extensive use of social media platforms for transactions and said the gang members provided customers links to their accounts for communication. They were supplying narcotics all over DHA and Clifton. As for the source of the narcotics, they have found out that they were buying the drugs from an area near Shahrah-e-Noor Jehan (Karachi).

Case Study 4 - Hacking into NADRA

The National Database and Registration Authority (NADRA) in Karachi, Pakistan announced a data breach in 2010. Thieves burglarized computers and other equipment. It hasn't been revealed whether disk encryption software was used to protect the contents of the stolen computers (Pakwired, 2016).

There is a possibility of linking to main NADRA servers. The breach happened at a branch office (Shah Faisal Colony Office, Karachi). However, ramifications of the breach may increase, as there is a possibility that the stolen computers could connect to the main NADRA servers, which would allow access to all records nationwide. Many lone hackers have managed to access the vulnerabilities of Pakistani websites, as a Turkish hacker penetrated into the NADRA and FIA official websites. In December 2012, a hacker who is named as Eboz, claimed to access the websites by just applying the simple method of SQL injection, one of the tactics to gain the administrative control access of a website (Pakwired, 2016).

Various countries are also found in spying other countries classified data present on the digital forum. It was revealed in August 2014 that, passport data related to Pakistani citizens which contained sensitive information and even biometric impressions was compromised. It was a breach by CIA and other US intelligence agencies as a part of their undercover project named 'HYDRA' (Pakwired, 2016).

Pakistani secret agencies have even discussed their concern over the unlawful access to data server by foreign secret services. Inter-Services Intelligence (ISI) in August 2014 censure the Israeli secret agency Mossad for their assay to hack sensitive data. Hostile countries, like India and Israel, etc., have been condemned multiple times for their covert attempts by the Government of Pakistan (Pakwired, 2016).

Case Study 5 - FBI's Most Wanted Cyber Criminal

In 2015, Pakistan Federal Investigation Agency (FIA), in a joint effort with FBI, USA, took a person in custody. The arrested cyber criminal was detained in Karachi, he was placed on top 10 most wanted criminals by the USA's government (Zaidi, 2015).

Mr. Noor Aziz Uddin, who unlawfully accessed the systems and deprived the victims of more than $50 million in November 2008 and April 2012. Further details on FBI's official website revealed that he had a reward of $50,000 on his capture. US authorities issued federal warrant for his arrest in several states like New Jersey and New York. He was charged for the act of conspiracy to commit online fraud, identity and personal information theft, and unlawful access to computer systems, etc., (Zaidi, 2015).

He was accused and convicted for establishing illegal telephone exchange which caused heavy losses. The victims were unaware of the respective threat and dangers included individuals, organizations, and government bodies, not only in the United States, but abroad.

Noor, along with a companion Farhan Arshad, unlawfully acquired access to private telephone systems. They crafted a trickery scheme generally known as 'international revenue share fraud'. They were illegally offering long distance telephone calls on expensive rates. This scam costed the real owners huge sum of losses, when they were billed heavily for unused services (Zaidi, 2015).

Case Study 6 - Reporter/Cyber Terrorist

Mr. Shahzeb Jillani is a Pakistani investigative reporter. He has served for Deutsche Welle as well as the BBC. He is currently engaged with Dunya News, a local Urdu news channel in Pakistan. He is accused of cyber terrorism by violating two criminal code provisions and four articles of Prevention of Electronic Crimes Act, 2016.

The case is lodged against him by a self-proclaimed 'loyal citizen' on 6th April, 2019. The plaintiff is a supreme court lawyer and he said that he was offended by Mr. Jillani's comment during a television broadcast on 8th December, 2017.

The head of RSF's Asia-Pacific desk, Mr.Daniel Bastard requested, "We urge the court to dismiss these charges against Shahzeb Jillani because, from the legal viewpoint, the case is completely inadmissible".

"Via the all-powerful Federal Investigation Agency, Pakistan's authorities are yet again manipulating the laws in order to silence a journalist who dared to cross a red line by criticizing certain institutions. It is shocking to see how, little by little, case by case, the Pakistani security agencies are tightening their vice in order to intimidate the entire media profession into censoring themselves."

Jillani was later freed on bail, shared with RSF that he is much surprised by the case. He is of the view that his recent story on missing persons, along with his 24th March, 2019 tweet, where he criticized the decision to decorate a senior military intelligence officer who was widely accused of political engineering during the national elections of Pakistan, 2018 are the reasons behind the case against him.

The real reason for the charges was in the run-up to those elections, RSF gave a detailed account of the various methods that the military establishment was using to put pressure on Pakistani media executives in order to impose its viewpoint and to silence reporters.

Jillani also shared with RSF that he has received little support from his news channel management. "The senior management has been told of the case, but their response is very cold". According to RSF's 2018 World Press Freedom Index, Pakistan is ranked 139th out of 180 countries.

Solutions and Recommendations

Mass awareness programs regarding cybercrime should be focused in Pakistan by engaging community and CBOs, NGOs, INGOs and cyber vigilantism. During the process of legislation regarding cybercrime expert opinion should be included, like criminologists, psychologists, sociologists, IT professionals, etc. As, in previous legislation, experts were not consulted. Cybercrime data should be maintained according to its nature and severity. It should be shared by Pakistani authorities with other countries. So, Pakistan could learn from the experience of other countries in this sphere.

The vulnerabilities of cyber world via seminars and workshops should be introduced to students. Victims of cybercrime should be given easy access to lodge a complain regarding online offenses. Special task force (i.e. cyber police) should be developed to especially ensure online routine checks at public places where internet is available. Any offensive (extremist) content, especially, with reference to race and religious hatred should be ban on websites. As, Pakistan is a very fragile state and such content can lead to civil disorder.

Private companies should develop a strong liaison with the Government of Pakistan's officials to ensure their internet services to an optimum level. The legal department in Pakistan should be equipped with the latest investigating technologies. In print as well as in electronic media, intellectuals should discuss cybercrime. E-transactions must be entered via websites that are authentic, and personal data (including passwords) should not be saved on public computers, as it is very unsafe. To effectively deal with cases of cybercrime, the respective judiciary, i.e. Session Court, District Courts, High Courts, as well as the Supreme Court of Pakistan must be given proper training.

Future Research Directions

Significant areas for conducting future research encompassing cybercrime via engaging qualitative, qualitative, or eclectic approach can be:

1. Electronic freedom in Pakistan.

2. Cyberterrorism in Pakistan.

3. Countering violent extremism in Pakistan.

4. Awareness regarding cybercrime in Pakistan.

Conclusion

There is no accurate way of understanding how prevalent cybercrime is in Pakistan. There exists no convenient way to identify how many people have been arrested or convicted of the cybercrime in Pakistan. That is partly, because of the way cybercrime law works in the Pakistani context. It was believed earlier that crimes related to cyberworld were very hard to investigate. All cybercrime could be theoretically charged, but as it is unlikely that consecutive sentence would be imposed to all respective offenses occurred before the legislation. It has been observed that there is an increase in people in Pakistan considering themselves to be the victim of a cybercrime. Cybercrime is one of the major problems with regards to technology in Pakistan, because it is growing by every second in a society where social networking and internet usage is becoming a norm. According to National Response Centre for Cyber Crime (NR3C) data set, in Pakistan, around 20% of the cyber related crimes are reported, the rest of the 80% remains unreported (Manzar, Tanveer, & Jamal, 2016). The forms in which a complaint can be registered are, online, form, fax, in writing and in person. To be able to lodge a complaint, the victim has to be inside Pakistan or the case cannot be entertained.

Differentiation in the categories of cybercrime in Pakistan is not that vivid. There is a difference between the kind of laws that are made in advanced countries and those of Pakistan. Cybercrime laws in Pakistan are very complex and even lodging a cybercrime incident is a hectic process. Pakistan is in dire need of making pertinent cyber laws. Pakistan is a developing country, but it has yet to develop cyber-norms, i.e. what is ethical in the Pakistani context and what is not. A low literacy rate as well as low employment rate further add to this dilemma. Therefore, the Pakistani government needs to focus on combating cybercrime, as it is a matter of great concern for upcoming generations in Pakistan.

References

Abaimov, S., & Martellini, M. (2020). *Cyber arms security in cyberspace*. Boca Raton, CRC Press. ISBN: 9780367853860

Austin, G. (2020). *National cyber emergencies: The return to civil defence*. London, Routledge. ISBN: 9780367360344

Azevedo, F. U. B. (2018). *Hackers exposed: Discover the secret world of cybercrime*. Independently published. ISBN-13: 978-1718124615

Bancroft, A. (2019). *The darknet and smarter crime: Methods for Investigating criminal entrepreneurs and the illicit drug economy (Palgrave studies in cybercrime and cybersecurity)*. Cham, Palgrave Macmillan. ISBN-13: 978-3030265113

Bandler, J., & Merzon, A. (2020). *Cybercrime investigations: A comprehensive resource for everyone*. Boca Raton, CRC Press. ISBN-13:978-0367196233

Benson, V., & McAlaney, J. (2019). *Emerging cyber threats and cognitive vulnerabilities* (1st ed.). Academic Press. ISBN-13: 978-0128162033

Carlson, C. T. (2019). *How to manage cybersecurity risk: A security leader's roadmap with open fair*. Universal Publishers. ISBN-13: 978-1627342766

Cuthbertson, A. (2016, January 11). Hackers take down Pakistan government websites on live radio. *Newsweek*.

Cuthbertson, A. (2018, November 12). Stolen data from 'almost all' Pakistan banks goes on sale on dark web. *The Independent*.

Cybercrime. (2020). In *Collins English Dictionary.*

https://www.collinsdictionary.com/dictionary/english/cybercrime

Cybercrime. (2020). In *Encyclopedia Britannica.* https://www.britannica.com/topic/cybercrime

Cybercrime. (2020). In *Merriam-Webster.* https://www.merriam-

webster.com/dictionary/cybercrime

Cybercrime. (2020). In *Oxford Advanced Learner's Dictionary.*

https://www.oxfordlearnersdictionaries.com/definition/english/cybercrime

Cybercrime. (2020). In *The Chambers Dictionary.*

https://www.cybercrimechambers.com/blog-web-jacking-117.php

Edwards, G. (2019). *Cybercrime investigators* (1ˢᵗ ed.). Hoboken, Wiley. ISBN-13: 978-

1119596288

Geo News. (2017, December 04). Hundreds of Pakistanis lose millions in major ATM skimming

fraud.

Gillespie, A. A. (2019). *Cybercrime: Key issues and debates*, London, Routledge. ISBN:

9781351010283

Graham, R. S., & Smith, S. K. (2019). *Cybercrime and digital deviance* (1ˢᵗ ed.). New York,

Routledge. ISBN: 9780815376316

Hudak, H. C. (2019). *Cybercrime (Privacy in the digital age).* North Star Editions. ISBN-13:

978-1644940815

Hufnagel, S., & Moiseienko, A. (2019). *Criminal networks and law enforcement: Global

perspectives on illegal enterprise.* London, Routledge.

Hutchings, A. (2013). *Theory and crime: Does it compute?*. Australia: Griffith University.

International Monetary Fund (2020). *World economic outlook database.*
https://www.imf.org/external/pubs/ft/weo/2019/02/weodata/index.aspx

Johansen, G. (2020). *Digital forensics and incident response: Incident response techniques and procedures to respond to modern cyber threats.* Birmingham, Packt Publishing. ISBN-13: 978-1838649005

Kim, P. (2018). *The hacker playbook 3: Practical guide to penetration testing.* Independently published. ISBN-13: 978-1980901754

Lavorgna, A. (2020). *Cybercrimes: Critical issues in a global context.* Springer. ISBN-13: 978-1352009118

Leukfeldt, R., & Holt, T. J. (2019). *The human factor of cybercrime.* London, Routledge. ISBN-13: 978-1138624696

Littler, M., & Lee, B. (2020). *Digital extremisms: Readings in violence, radicalisation and extremism in the online space.* Cham, Springer Nature Switzerland AG. ISBN13: 9783030301378

Lusthaus, J. (2012). Trust in the world of cybercrime. *Global Crime, 13*(2), 71-94.

Manzar, U., Tanveer, S., & Jamal, S. (2016, June). *The incidence of cybercrime in Pakistan.* 10.13140/rg.2.1.1641.9448

Marion, N. E., & Twede, J. (2020). *Cybercrime: An encyclopedia of digital crime.* Santa Barbara, ABC-CLIO. ISBN-13: 978-1440857348

Marsh, B., & Melville, G. (2019). *Crime, justice and the media*. London, Routledge. ISBN: 9780429432194

Martellozzo, E., & Jane, E. A. (2017). *Cybercrime and its victims*. London, Routledge.

Pakwired. (2016, January 13). How secure are NADRA's critical information systems?. https://pakwired.com/how-secure-are-nadras-critical-information-systems/

Perwaiz, S. B. (2017, September 19). Four held as cops bust gang using social media for drug sales. *The News International*.

Reporters Without Borders. (2019, April 16). *Pakistani investigative reporter accused of "cyber-terrorism"*.

Sangster, M. (2020). *No safe harbor: The inside truth about cybercrime and how to protect your business*. Vancouver, Page Two. ISBN-13: 978-1989603420

Schober, S. N., & Schober, C. W. (2019). *Cybersecurity is everybody's business: Solve the security puzzle for your small business and home*. ScottSchober.com Publishing. ISBN-13: 978-0996902267

Steinberg, J. (2019). *Cybersecurity for dummies (For dummies computer/tech)*. Hoboken, John Wiley & Sons. ISBN: 9781119560326

Troia, V. (2020). *Hunting cyber criminals: A hacker's guide to online Intelligence gathering tools and techniques*. Indianapolis, Wiley. ISBN-13: 978-1119540922

Willems, E. (2019). *Cyberdanger: Understanding and guarding against cybercrime*. Springer International Publishing. ISBN:978-3-030-04531-9

Yar, M., & Steinmetz, K. F. (2019). *Cybercrime and society* (3rd ed.). SAGE Publications Ltd. ISBN-13: 978-1526440648

Zaidi, M. (2015, February 14). FBI's most wanted cyber criminal arrested in Karachi. *Dawn.* https://www.dawn.com/news/1163584

Additional Readings

1. Government of Pakistan. Economic Survey of Pakistan, 2017. Retrieved from http://www.finance.gov.pk/survey_1617.html

2. Government of Pakistan. Electronic Transactions Ordinance, 2002. Retrieved July 28, 2018, from http://www.pakistanlaw.com/eto.pdf

3. Government of Pakistan. Prevention of Electronic Crimes Act, 2016. Retrieved August 12, 2018, from http://www.na.gov.pk/uploads/documents/1470910659_707.pdf

4. Government of Pakistan. Provisional Summary Results of 6th Population and Housing Census - 2017. Pakistan Bureau of Statistics. Retrieved September 19, 2018, from https://bytesforall.pk/

5. Imam, A. L. (2012 December). *Cyber crime in Pakistan: Serious threat but no laws!.*

6. Internet World Stats. (2018). Retrieved from https://www.internetworldstats.com/asia/pk.htm

7. Investigation for Fair Trial Act, 2013. Retrieved September 11, 2018, from http://www.na.gov.pk/uploads/documents/1361943916_947.pdf

8. Leukfeldt, E. R. (2014). Cybercrime and social ties. *Trends in Organized Crime, 17*(4), 231-249.

9. Momein, F. A., & Brohi, M. N. (2010). Cybercrime and internet growth in Pakistan. *Asian Journal of Information Technology, 9* (1), 1 - 4.

10. National Response Centre for Cyber Crime (NR3C). Retrieved August 18, 2018, from http://www.nr3c.gov.pk/cybercrime.html

Key Terms

1. **Cybercrime:** The use of a computer to commit a crime.

2. **Cyberterrorism:** The use of Information and Communication Technology to cause grave disruption or pervasive fear.

3. **Cyberworld:** The world of inter-computer communication.

4. **Cyber security:** Security on the internet.

5. **Hacking:** To gain unauthorized access to data in a system or computer.

Publisher: Eliva Press SRL

Email: info@elivapress.com

Eliva Press is an independent publishing house established for the publication and dissemination of academic works all over the world. Company provides high quality and professional service for all of our authors.

Our Services:
Free of charge, open-minded, eco-friendly, innovational.

-All services are free of charge for you as our author (manuscript review, step-by-step book preparation, publication, distribution, and marketing).
-No financial risk. The author is not obliged to pay any hidden fees for publication.
-Editors. Dedicated editors will assist step by step through the projects.
-Money paid to the author for every book sold. Up to 50% royalties guaranteed.
-ISBN (International Standard Book Number). We assign a unique ISBN to every Eliva Press book.
-Digital archive storage. Books will be available online for a long time. We don't need to have a stock of our titles. No unsold copies. Eliva Press uses environment friendly print on demand technology that limits the needs of publishing business. We care about environment and share these principles with our customers.
-Cover design. Cover art is designed by a professional designer.
-Worldwide distribution. We continue expanding our distribution channels to make sure that all readers have access to our books.

www.elivapress.com